BLACK

BLACK

TO THE ROOTS

GEORGE BOSTON RHYNES

Lagrange Georgia

BLACK TO THE ROOTS
Copyright © 2024 by GEORGE BOSTON RHYNES

Printed in the United States of America. No part of this publication may be used or reproduced, stored in a retrieval system, transmitted in any form or by any means-electronic, mechanical, photocopy, recording, or any other except for brief quotations in printed reviews, without the publisher's prior written permission.

iSeebookz Publishing
Suite 137B Commerce Ave #300
Lagrange GA 30241

Editor: Y.D. Rowland
Cover design: George B. Rhynes & iSeebookz Publishing Services
Interior design assistant: D.J. Rowland

ISBN 979-8-9854863-8-4

First Edition
10 9 8 7 6 5 4 3 2 1

First Printing, 2024

This book is Dedicated to...

Mrs. Eliza Bryant, my grandmother who had only a third or fourth grade education, but a washpot full of Love, Wisdom, and Understanding. It was by her navigating abilities that kept me afloat as I travel the rough seas of this life. To my mother Evalina Rhynes, -her enduring love for God to follow in His way- I have my being in this living world. To my children thank you for our true loving connection and your support as we give honor to your mother and my late wife, Ruby. To everyone who has made my life a journey of continual learning, your watering interactions gave root and I stand today. Thank you.

1

The Tower of Power, The Man of the Hour

The Tower of Power The Man of the Hour

{symbolism}

The Tower of Power! The man of the hour,
The force, the truth, the creator, the real H-Bomb.
No one before him, no one after him
The Tower of Power, The spirit,
The all-knowing! GOD!

No puff, no fluff, no fuss, the real deal
Burst into Earth's atmosphere to heal!
No detonation is needed! No name can describe him,
Time can't stop him, Bullets can't penetrate him,
No force can destroy him.
No missiles can reach him, no educator can teach him
No man can contain him,
No child or baby can play on his sympathy!

He is, He was, and always will be, The Tower Of Power
The man of the hour, the real BOMB!
No one before him, no one after Him,
No one, No two, No hundred trillion can betray him!
He was, He is, the pill that heal the ill,
And transforms it into a thrill!

He never knew Muslim, Islam, or Judaism.
He never knew Christianity, nor taught denominations
He just gave the world love, power and a sound mind
And He sent this universal message,
To all mankind for all times...

"Love thy neighbor as you love yourself,"

Why would He teach such a Universal Message?

Because he wanted us to have and enjoy
The same things that he himself enjoys!

The Tower of Power, the Man of the Hour
The God, The Force, The Truth, The Infinity, the real BOMB!
That explodes 100 trillion tons of TNT,
Called the love connection!

Combining hearts to hearts,
Thereby creating a Universal Love Affair
Among the brotherhood and sisterhood of man and mankind!
The Tower of Power, the Man of the Hour GOD!

2

I Am Black

I Am Black

I am Black; Blacker than blue Black,
So Black, that I cannot back back
Without backing back, into the blackness of myself!

I am Black, So black, that people hate me, simply because I am black,
I came through the back door; to reach the front door,
Then sat on the back of the bus without causing any fuss!
I am Black, and I drive a Black Cadillac.

The rhythm in my twist, ignites the nucleus of my mind,
That causes a love sensation; to run down into my spine,
That makes any woman change her mind,
So when I make contact, in the blackness of her womb,
Though she be Black, White, Red, Yellow, or Brown,
My Blackness will linger around for a lifetime!
Because I am Black, Never was a Nigger!

Negro, Colored,
Af-ri-can American or any less than
The White Man Or any other man!

I am Black, Blacker than blue Black,
Blacker than the Ace of Spades!
So Black, that even my thoughts are black,
So Black, that I am disliked, simply because I'm Black,
Yet, I made Little Black Sambo, acknowledge
That he was only painted, Black!

I am Black, So Black, that when I looked back,
Through my rearview mirror on my Black Cadillac,
All I see is Black!

When I was held back, kicked back,
Laid back, knocked back,
Went back, turned back, jumped back,
Pushed so far back into the back,
That my Black Doctor—
Prescribed me a couple of Standbacks!
That left me humped back,
But I took the hump off my back,
And became a running back, halfback, tailback, full back,
Then I bounced back, so they crowned me
The Black Quarterback!

Now, I just keep coming back,
Because I am, that I am,
In the likeness of my Black Creator!
For he is the generator, that keeps my Blackness intact!

So never, try to confuse me,
By calling me, an Af-ri-can, American,
For that name is reserved for the White Man,
Who left the Motherland of Africa, and came to America,
Then blended in, with his white skin, and kin!
So yes! Call him, an Af-ri-can American!

But I am Black, Like Solomon,
Black Like the Rose Of Sharon!
Black like the Black Stone of MECCA,
Black, like the original earth,
Beneath the Walling Wall, Black,
Like charcoal that heats the stove,
Black like the Black hole in outer space!

So yes! Call me Black, because Black is God's Delight!
This is why! I keep coming back, and can't be stopped,
My Truth! Wisdom, knowledge and understanding
Will prevail regardless of how they treat me!

So come on, Turn on your brightest lights in the West,
Only to be blinded By the Ancient Knowledge
Of the original Black Light!

So come on, give Blackness a swirl,
And I will keep coming back because
I am Black, stable, beautiful,
Intact and I like that, so this is why---
I keep coming back,
Because I am, Black!

Fact or Fiction, disapprove me---if you can.
My ancestors came from Africa, Black.
I was born Black,
I was Black yesterday, I am Black now!
And I will be Black Tomorrow!

My great, great grandmother, told me
That when I'm dead, I'll be Black,

So for me to become anything; other than a Black Man,
Is to become---my brother's Uncle—TOM{*sell-out*}!
Power to the people, now pass it on.
Peace!

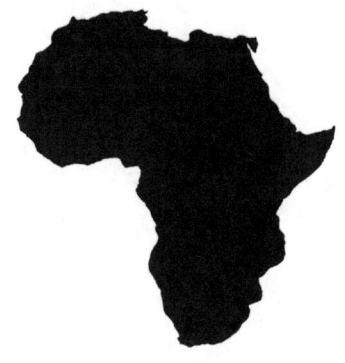

3

R.H.I.P. Or Rank Has Its Privileges

R.H.I.P. Or Rank Has Its Privileges

Upon being commissioned,
I was awarded two bars of gold (2nd Lt.)
With it came authority I was told, but found myself serving wine.

In due time, I was awarded two bars of silver (1st Lt),
With them came authority---I was told,
Only to feel barred in and painted over.

Later I was awarded two double bars of silver (Captain),
With Them came greater authority I was told,
But I never saw the change--Only Bars.

And beyond the bars, I beheld a golden leaf (Major)
With it came yet greater authority, I was told,
But a leaf on a tree is nothing to be
For you see the birds they became quite fond of me.

So I reached out and caught the bird by his wings (Colonel)
And with this bird came ultimate authority---I was told,
So I went out and tried to fly---only to be blinded by a star.

So as I traveled through the mist, I caught the shining star,
And with it came infinite authority---I was told,
And I kept receiving stars until I heard a voice from heaven,
Say, Sir, you left the gold, passed through silver
Caught the eagle by his wings, and now you're playing
Around with the stars (General).

But Sir, possessing the stars don't make you boss
Just puts you in a position to be first to fall,
You see except you repent and believe
That Jesus is the Christ, the Son of the living God
You can by no means enter into the next level.

The Voice gave the Stars (General)
A sharp (hand) salute and departed---and until this day
Generals at all levels of Command must stand at attention,
When in the presents of the Ultimate Power, GOD!

4

The Little Acorn

I'm just a little acorn destined for the skies,
and neither rain nor sleet,
Nor the threat of destruction shall keep
this little acorn,
from saying it's peace.

Yes, I fell from a tree of destiny to a spot,
I called my own,
while reaching out with all I had,
trying to remain,
but with no success.

Now I'm traveling in a stream,
and on my way,
To some unknown land,
where I'll stop and commence to grow.
But I'll never be happy
for only the skies will satisfy,
This little acorn desires.

Because I'm just a little acorn
Destined for the skies,
and neither rain nor sleet,
Nor the threat of destruction
shall keep this little acorn, from saying it peace.
For I too, Am destined to become a tree of destiny!

5

A Falling Star

      A
         F
            A
               L
                  L
                     I
                        N
                           G

STAR
Is only a reminder
That we all must go sometime
To a place where we'll be weighed
For running a race---to show the Maker
That his grace, was not a waste!

6

The World's Greatest Traveler

The World's Greatest Traveler

I served in the souls of men; I walked life's restless journey,
I traveled around the world and I placed Truth in its center.
I measured the earth, with a span of my hand,
I dipped my fingers into the Mediterranean Sea.
And I've seen men, of every kindred and nation.
I walked the streets, with the finest of women,
And sin never entered my being, nor did it approach,
The boarders of my mind!
And in due time, I stepped out of nowhere,
Yet, from somewhere and declared, that I am that I am!
And by the power and authority within,
I stretched forth my hand and drew a line,
That no man could bend.
I leaned over and from the dust of the ground,
I created Man on the Trestleboard of my own hand.
Then lifted up my head and declared, My eyes are in every place,
Beholding the evil and the good.

I am the originator of life, I spoke,
And the light shined out of darkness,
Grass grew, birds flew and sang the joys of their beginning,
But I alone the infinite,
Residing in total darkness, hail and conceal,
The beginning and the ending,
Yes! By the power and authority within,
I stepped out of nowhere,
Yet from somewhere and declared, That I am, That I am.

7

The Religious Box

The Religious Box

Please, stay inside your box.
If you feel the urge to leave your box,
Please ignore it, by any means necessary.

If you, must move outside of your box,
Be sure to return, to the same spot,
Before you left your box.

But it is, Always best to never leave your box,
This is the highest calling, of a good,
Faithful and dedicated patriot.

If you find, that your box has been moved at anytime,
For any reason, be sure to move in the same direction,
As your box, until you find your box,
And get back, inside immediately!

Moreover, if for any reason, you should misplace, your box,
Go to your nearest religious institution,
Political or government Agency!

And they, will gladly, issue, you a new Box, free of charge,
But whatever you do, never remain outside your Box,
Long enough for independent thinking--- to take place.

This can be extremely dangerous, and destructive,
For both you and your Box.

So never, ever question, why, you must stay inside your Box.

Be quiet, and NEVER ask,
Why your religious, political, economic,
and government institutions are happy, as long as you;
Remain inside the Box; they designed for you!

And never forget, that as long as you are inside your Box,
You are safe; loved; secure, happy, a real patriot,
And truly loved, by everybody!

So there is no need to think for yourself,
Your family, community, state, nation and world,
Your security is in the Box, It has eliminated,
The need to read, write, educate yourself, and your family.

Everything, has been provided for you in the Box.

So stay inside your Box,
You are on your way to success,
And never question your happiness.

8

Hip Me To The Level Of Your Intelligence

Only Truth, was able to hip ME to your level of intelligence,
So to the hustler's of religion and political politicians,
You cannot continue to pimp the people, once they learn,
The knowledge of your pimping.
So to the preacher, and politician,
Who pimps the people, preaching from the paper;
In the pulpit and from the White House Script!

Making the people pay, for that particular day,
for the message you preach, you better beware-- and pray,
That the people remain stupid!

Because, you cannot continue, pimping the people,
When the people are told, and you are exposed,
Concerning the tricks of your trade.

Because people united, and informed, will never be defeated,
And speaking Truth to power,
Brings about the beauty of a flower,
Like the cries, and desires of the elders, will bring out,
The aspirations of the child.

Thereby, helping them to realize, that bombs was not designed,
Or made, to bring about peace, but rather to kill,
Like a plane was made to fly, like a car, was made to drive,
Like a cell phone, was made to be talked on,
And that the voice in the wilderness,
Will sooner, or later be heard.

So there is nothing, you can say or due,
When Truth is on the prowl.

I said it once, and I'll say it twice,
Only Truth was able to hip me,
To the level, of your intelligence.

So to the hustler's of religion, politics and a few others.
You cannot continue pimping, the people,
Once they learn the knowledge of your pimping!

So, to those who pimps the people preaching from the paper,
in the pulpit, making the people pay, you better beware,
and pray that the people remain stupid.

Now this is, the message from me--to you!

Only Truth was able to hip me, to the level of your intelligence!
So now, in CONCLUSION, I'm, through--with you!

So brother preachers, political politicians and others,
stop pimping the people, from the paper, in the pulpit,
And making them pay, for that particular day.

Because GOD, has something to say, Peace, Please!

9

Pointing The Way

PSALMS 68:31   **MATTHEW 2:15**

Pointing The Way

When men were enslaved, in the days of old,
I knew then, it were against El Shaddai's way,
So I came from the Land of Cush, to help point the way.
Through pain and tears, I bore the mark of an Orphan child.

Though my history was concealed,
Making it impossible, for me to see, from whence I came.

But In due time, El Shaddai opened my eyes,
And raised my hand in victory,
To ensure that I, help point the way.

I was shackled in chains, and denied my fame,
Even told my brain had been profaned.
But I took it in stride, while feeling the pain,
That pierced my side.

You see, I came from the Land of Cush (Alkebulan)
To help point the way.
Yet, many still deny, that I was made from the dust of the clay.
But rather believe, I came from some other,
Mysterious and ungodly way.

But today, here I stand, with nothing to say,
But that I came from Ethiopia (Africa),
To help point the way.

10

The Heavenly Bird

There is a bird in the sky, flying high
For you and I, and He has traveled a many of miles,
Just to say you're my child, and I know he will lead you,
To his home bye and bye.

So if you abide in the Master's will (God),
Surely He will lead you upon the hill.
The hill that Moses had to climb,
The one that Joshua had to come down.

Yes, there is a bird somewhere, Even closer than the sky,
And He will take you, to his home bye and bye!

11

What Manner Of Man Is This

What Manner Of Man Is This

Once deep within, the darken continent of Africa,
The Mother Land of Ancient and Modern Man,
When men lived beneath, the sun-lit skies,
Walking in harmony, with Mother Nature,
And paying tribute to Eel Shaddi,
The only true and living God,
Of all the worlds-both known and unknown.

Until a cry was heard, the shock that shocked,
And rocked that entire African nation,
For a remnant of chosen specimens, to come forth,
And share its naturalness, with a world unknown,
To set sail for the western world.

His wisdom, and knowledge, predated that of modern man.

He was mistakenly called, a jungle bunny,
Uncivilized, and incapable of learning (some proclaimed),

Yet, In the midst of this pessimistic idea,
He became the craft men,
And artisans, that help shape every civilization,
known to ancient and modern man.

It was this Nigger, colored, negro, coon, or
Burrhead, Shine Black African American,
That mastered the art of brass, As Tubal Cain,
And from his creation,
Music was a part of his total being, As Zila.

He discovered cities and hamlets, he even left his mark in Egypt,
Upon the pyramids in Gizah, he fought in civil wars,
Against his own brothers, not knowing,
From whence, he himself had come.

He was seen, as a tall dark stranger, marching up to Zion,
With A halo above his head, and no one, dared to approach him.
He stood at the altar, but no one gave attendance,
He was called a boy, by those who would try, and tear him apart.

He was often tried, by the forces of evil, but never denied,
By men of Truth, that he was special, in the eyes,
Of Almighty God. His lips was thick, his noise was broad,
His skin was darker, Than the Ace of Spade.

His cable tow extended backwards, into the dusk of the ground,
To the exact point--wherein God himself said,
Let there be light, anchored deep down into the mind,
Of Almighty God, who resided in total darkness.

Much Like the original man; and from that darkened house,
God himself said, let us make man, to replenish and reform,
The nations of the world.

For over 400 years, he walked in total darkness,
seeing only through dreams and visions,
Set forth by the hand of the infinite,
Waiting for his time to be laid,
and fitted into the temple of Truth, to purge the unclean,
And make straight the crooked path.

He was commissioned, to build a new ark,
To a modern day Goliath,
To march around the walls of Jericho,
Of a modern day Jericho.

And in due time, by divine providence, he was released,
From the belly of the beast, and called to march,
Through the Red Sea, at high tides, when the waters were fierce,
And the cloud of man rained down blood,
Upon his people, and no one reported his major events,
Into the annals of history.

That in future years, it might stimulate his circulation,
And be accepted by the European Nations of the world.

But for too long, he was held in a strange land,
Among strange people for over 450 years in North America,
Cutting stones, picking cotton, making brick without straw,
Cutting timber from the forest, of a modern day Lebanon,
Building up a civilization, that he himself could not enjoy.

He watched, as the birds drink water,
From a fountain that he himself built,
But he had to drink his water from a creek.

So he turned, and looked toward the east, for divine direction,
In search of peace, and relief,
And heard the answer, that his forebears,
Had long sought for.

And it came, in the form of a riddle, saying whom I set free,
Is free in deed--for Truth on the scaffold...

Therefore, go on my son, and let it be, let it be,
And soon the world, will come to see,
Just how much, you mean to me.

Yes, Yes, Yes, says my God, I was with thee in the land of Africa,
Abroad the ships that brought them over, those who jumped,
And were thrown overboard and made their home within,
The ocean flow, I was there.

I was there, when you lived among the native American,
When those who died under the hand of heavy task masters.
And to those of you who assisted in your deliverance,
Our God will see you through,
For the best is yet to come!

the father and the son...

12

The Dot Of Truth

The Dot Of Truth

There is a dot that marks the spot
Some say it was hidden; way back behind the veil
Wrapped in mystery; lies and half truths!

But before there was a William Shakespeare
Before there was a King James I. of England
Before there was a Christopher Columbus
Before there was a President George Washington
Before there were a Pope Paul of Rome
Or a John the Revelator
There was a dot that marked the spot!

Way, way back Before Apostle Paul
Had his Damascus Road Experience
Before Jesus was crucified on the cross of Calvary
Before John Baptized Jesus of Nazareth
And the wise men ever saw the star in the East
There was a dot that marked the spot!

Before Meshach, Shadrack, And Abednego
Walked through the flames of fire
Before Joshua marched around the Walls of Jericho
Before Job showed up for his interview
In the Land Of Uz With God And the Devil
There was a dot that marked the spot!

Before The Heavy Hand of God Fell upon Ezekiel
That made him speak to dry bones in the valley
Before Moses led the children of Israel through the Red Sea
And into the Promised Land.

Before Noah built the Ark prior to the Great Flood
Before Cain slew his brother Abel
Before God scooped up a dust of clay
And He said, let us make man
There was a dot that marked the spot!

THE PLUMBLINE OF TRUTH

13

Two Columns Of Life

Two Columns Of Life

The old man discovered two columns of life
He never named them;
He just learned from them both.
However, as he grew older and wiser,
He called the one to his left beauty and the one on his right
Strength.

He later said that every man, woman, boy, or girl will sooner or
Later find themselves traveling through these two columns of life.
Many will bypass them and pay no attention to them
Others will cling to the one and deny the other.

Yet, there are those who will cling to them both
And never depart from either.
Whichever or whatever action one may take
No one can erase the fact that they exist!

These pillars or columns may appear to be made of wood
Brick, stone, clay or even gold, but there are more than these
For when one looks beyond the shadow of what appears
And look deeper into the power of Truth;

Crying out to be known from the depths of these two columns
For they represent Right And Wrong, up and down
In and out: Black and White
East And West; South And North
God and Satan; Fire and Water; Wet and Dry
Light and Darkness; Success and Failure
Top and Bottom Backwards and Forward; Male and Female

Sister and Brother; Sight and Blindness; Strength And Weakness
Win and Loose; Freedom and Slavery; Me and You!

The columns of Strength and Beauty is the two columns
That we all sooner or later shall pass through
this gate Called The Columns of Life!

Some may approach them because of fear
But make no mistake my friend
They do appear!

14

The Traveling Man

THE PLUMBLINE OF TRUTH

The Traveling Man

A man only known as the traveler
Was wondering in the darkness of night
When he stumbled upon a house
He was broke; hungry and destitute
So he knocked on the door
This door was called knowledge
And freely it opened
Of its own freewill and accord!

But the traveler took an honest
Self-examination of himself
And realized that he was not worthy
To enter (into the door of knowledge!)

So, he took a seat near the outer door
Where he beheld a Little Black Book
And as he reached for the Little Black Book
The door slammed shut
Then wondered;
If The Little Black Book Wasn't the key!

So, He took the book
And after reading the Book
He returned to the door of knowledge
And There he knocked again,
And to his surprise
His eyes, were opened
And the door was closed no more!

15

The Tub

Every tub sits
On its own bottom!
But He who owns
The Land Beneath the Tub
Has control over
How the tub will be used!

16

Words Of Wisdom

SYMBOL OF WISDOM, CREATIVITY AND THE COMPLEXITIES OF LIFE

Words Of Wisdom

"Knowledge Within Knowledge"
To truly be in possession of knowledge
One must look deep into knowledge
And understand who resides
In the house (of knowledge!)
There are seven words
Nine letters or
Characters!

The
House of Knowledge
Rests upon seven pillars that make up
The true foundation of the nine characters!
This house possesses seven rooms or areas of habitation!
Know Can be found in the living room of this house!
No; Can Be found in the doorway of this house!
Owl; The symbol of wisdom can be found in the den of this house!
Now; Can be found in the kitchen of this house!
Led; Can be found in the Dining Room of this house!
Ledge; Can be found in the Master Bedroom of this house!
Edge; Can be found in the Hallway of this house!

What house am I speaking of?
It is the house of knowledge!
And to possess her is to know her!
And to know her is to understand her!
And to understand her is to acknowledge
What lives within her heart!

Wisdom speaks here

KNOWLEDGE DEFINED

- *Know - To have a clear perception or understanding of, be sure of, or be well informed about. (To Know The Facts).*
- *No - Not ever, not in any degree; not at all. Opposite Of Yes.*
- *Now - At the present time; at this moment.*
- *Owl - Any of an order of birds of prey found throughout the world.*
- *Led - To show the way to or direct the course of by going before or along with, conduct, guide.*
- *Ledge - A projecting ridge of rocks.*
- *Edge - The thin, sharp, cutting part of a blade.*

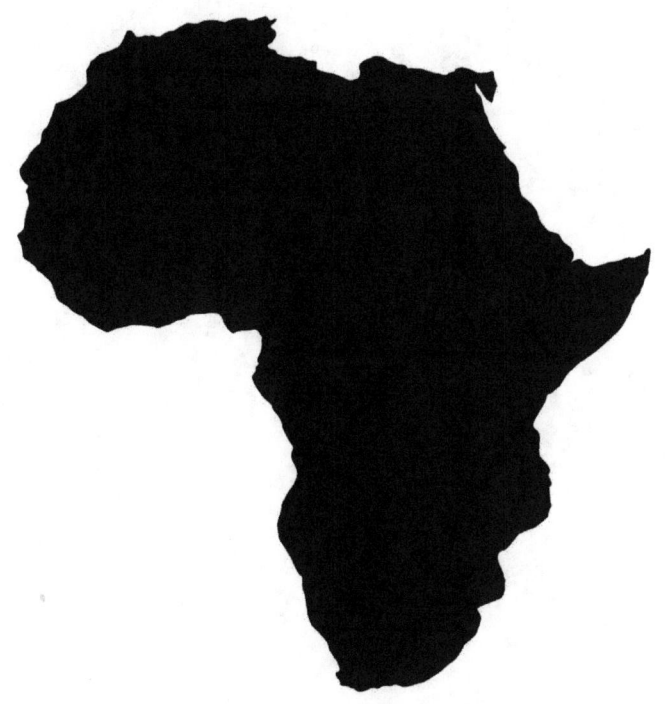

17

Wisdom Of The Wise Or Falsehood In Disguise

Wisdom Of The Wise Or Falsehood In Disguise

Wisdom of a true man
Is as a flat rock rolling along.

Many men have seen it
But only a few will confess it
And of the few that confess it
Some Will forget it
Or deny they ever saw it
From being mocked and scorned
By men that saw it
But couldn't believe it.

Yet there are those
Who have both seen and confessed to it
And Have attempted to destroy it
Because they could not forget it.

While some claim to have seen it
And will confess to it
Although they have never seen it
But will kill
If you try to destroy it.

But a wise man
He can see it
And confess to it
But never will he kill to protect it
Because he has seen it

And knows within his mind
His Soul and very being
That no man can take it.

So of all the men
That have seen it
And confessed to it
Has Lost it
But the wise man - has kept it
Because he believed it.

18

Read To Learn & Pass It On To A Friend

Closer than a brother

He who talks behind someone's back.
Will soon be required to turn around!

The way you go is the way you choose
And the day you tarry could
be the day you lose!

The shortest route
Is not always the safest way home!
 And even then,
Be careful how you blow your horn.

Beware of men
who drive nice cars
They may also drive large
nails in women's heads!

An empty wagon makes
a lot of noise
And one loaded with
cotton balls
makes little difference

It's not how much money
You make-
That makes one rich;
But what you do
With what you have!

Train up a child in the
way he should go,
And when he is old,
he will not depart from it!

Women are like the sun that shines brightest
In the morning! And in the evening,
they are no less brighter. But what you see is defined
by what's within your own head!

A foolish woman destroys her home.
But the wise woman builds hers!

Life and death are in the power of the tongue
And the way you use it will determine how far you go in life.
To control the tongue is to destroy
a deadly poison within the body.

A house can never become a home
Unless you first lay a good foundation in love.

Love is something that man cannot make.
And at best, he can only have sex. But God is love,
And God is something that no man is capable of making!

19

Trust

Trust

You can't trust a man because a man's a liar;
But God will stand by you until the day you die;
And When you're dead, He has just begun;
You see! I came home on the morning train;
But I couldn't find no-body there;

They say my mother she's dead, And my sister been gone;
And my brother has been dead ---long time ago;

Now tell me people, what I'm going to do;
Cause I'm just as lonesome,
As the loneliest man;
The loneliest man in all the world!

Now I have done tried to kill myself, But here I am, dangling
From the end of a rope swinging from a Chinaberry tree;

And if this rope don't hurry and break,
Then I'm going to hell; To my promised land!

Somebody please tell me What I am going to do;
Well, I called on my friends, but they didn't answer
So I called on the man Who made the earth;
And the heaven above; I said Oh Lord.
Won't you help me now?
This rope is getting tight;

My life is getting short; I said Oh Lord,
Help me win this fight.

The rope began to break
And I began to shake; I said, Oh Lord,
I know you're great!

Well, you can't trust a man, because a man is a liar
But my God will stand by you -
Until the day you die!

20

Lady of the Night

The Lady of the Night

The Lady of the Night
She struts the street
From strip to strip,
She aims her eyes like the Eagle when he flies.

As she looks down upon her prey
And zeros in upon the one she plans to let take her in
Then she presents him with a kiss,
As a token of her love.

Yet her kisses are but a deadly blow,
So up in the morning like the rising sun,
She gets up and goes her way.

And from whence He came if remembered,
Is only for a night.

Yet if they should bow and come to light,
God will in no wise cast them out.

21

Loving Man Blues

Loving Man Blues

If you,
Don't love me baby
I just want to lie down and die
I wouldn't kill myself
Because that wouldn't inflict - enough pain
To show you just how much, I love you baby!

So if you,
Don't love me baby, That's OK!
But let me tell you
What I'm about to say
I'm going to climb up into the tallest mountain

But I won't jump down
Because there is not enough pain
In the world to equal, my love for you.

So if you,
Don't love me baby; I'd jump into a den
Of rattlesnakes, let them bite me
All over my head, and under my neck

But I don't believe, God, nor Jesus
Would let me die
Because they knows, the depths
Of my love for you!

So if you,
Don't love me baby, and if you don't mind

Please tell me NOW, or forever hold your peace

So if you,
Don't love me Girl, That's OK:
I'll just bow down, on my knees,
And pray to God, until eternity!
Because that's, just how much
I love you baby!

22

Black Man Eclipse

The Eclipse Of The Black Man

Black man! Open up your eyes!
The house of incarceration
And indoctrination is being expanded;
By Bogus powers of this generation.

As they seek to sap your powers,
Transforming our minds
And destroying our very soul;
Down to the 3rd and 4th generation.

Black, yellow and brown; wake up
To a new reality of the times.
Don't you ever worship a god,
That does not look like you.
Never, ever walk a thousand miles
For anything when you can ride.

Never fear, mistrust, undermine
Or kill, each other, for this ---is
The New Trick of the Slave Master.
That has the potential of killing all of us!

So never forget to teach your people,
Regardless, of whom they marry,
That they cannot be placed on probation
As long as they are in possession, of true education.

So tell your children, to tell their children
To never, ever submit to indoctrination
Because, it only leads
to the incarceration of your God,

Given mind.

So stand bold, stand strong
Take care of your own, stand your ground;
Stay your distance, because you are
The Black Seed that God needs.

So In conclusion, never ever, forget,
That without you, there would be no beginning
And without you, there will be no ending.
So always, stand strong
And take care of your own!

Walk The Line

Lord, I'm living,
In these trying times,
But I'm moving on; No one before me;
No one behind me, Yet I walk the line.

Through toil and tears, I bored the mark;
Of an orphan child, Yet, I walk the line;
Trying to find, Me a better home.

No one before me, No one behind me;
Yet, I travel on.
As I travel, To And fro,
Wading through this old veil of tears,
Satan meet me wherever I go,
Yet, I walk the line.

No one before me, No one behind me,
Yet, I travel on, Praying to my JESUS,
To help me walk the line.

Cause I'm living in, These trying times,
But I'm moving on, No one before me,
No One behind me, Yet, I walk the line.

All because my JESUS, Helps me walk the line.

THE PLUMBLINE OF TRUTH

FERTILIZER FOR THOUGHT QUOTE

*Two heads may be
Better than one!
But never forget which one
Belongs to You!*

George Boston Rhynes

24

Fertilized Thoughts

When I am A Man,
A man-
A blacksmith I'll be
If I can, and I can
And then I will trout
Around the square,
To see if its right,
When I'm A Man!

The Foolish Man's Eyes
Are on the things of the world.
But the wise man eyes is in his head!

Always keep your hands to yourself
  Because you're going to need them one day!

If you cannot find a husband,
    Then stop looking, and one will find you!

    Forty-five nickels
  And forty-five dimes
     A baby like you
     Is hard to find!

Rainbow in the morning
   take a warning
Rainbow in the evening
 The rain is leaving!

What goes up must come down
And what goes in must come out
Then again, what goes around
Comes around.
But that doesn't mean
You will be around to see it!

Give a man a fish
And he will eat for a day.
Teach him to fish,
And he will eat for a lifetime;
But Only if he owns the land beneath the pond.

You can get fired from your job
But fire will cause everybody to leave!

The way I go
Is the way I choose
And the day I tarry
Could be the day I lose….

And it's not how much you know
That makes you smart
But how smart you know you are!

25

Altar Of Truth An Easter Thought

Altar Of Truth (An Easter Thought)
Deuteronomy 12:3

The altar of truth
Is the foundation
Upon which all Altar's lay.

It has stood the test of time
Though sometimes hidden
By a bleak mist of sin
Yet' forever imitating the light
From the master's hand.

With its secrets
And unfolded mysteries
It continues to speak
To all that bow.

And forever cutting
Both left and right,
Those that reject and defy
The foundations upon which it lay.

So up from a mists
Out of a darkened night
Budded a little horn
To So shine in the night.

But sinful men sought darkness
And killed that light,

And just-when sinful men thought
They had done. the little horn in
The Grand Master of creation
He stepped in,
And rendered a helping hand.

Bringing forth,
From deep within
A darken tomb,
An everlasting flame
That could not be contained,
Ascended and descended
Into the underworld,
Met Satan and
Took the key The past key,
And the master key,
Then set on the right hand
Of the most high, and almighty
To wait,
For you and I..

So today,
Men and women of truth
Cannot lie,
And say that Easter,
Is about Easter Eggs
And Easter bunnies

But rather that Jesus of Nazareth
Arose from the grave
With palms of Victory
In his hand.

And this is why
We celebrate Easter my friend.

26

A Personal Talk with Jesus

A Personal Talk with Jesus

I'm down
Here Lord Jesus!
In this modern land
Nothing but trouble
Trouble on every hand.

Now there goes my friend
With a gun in his hand-

He says
That he hates his neighbor
But he say
That I'm his friend.

Now that forces me to wonder
Is he carrying that gun for me?

Because how can he say
That he love me
When his neighbor is my friend!

So let us not condemn this world saying
There ain't no love in here,
For God made this world
And HE made it out of love!

27

The Great Meeting

The Great Meeting

If I could meet
Old Master Jesus
I'd catch him by the hand
And lead him to the Southside
And let him rest a while.

I'd let him see the poverty
That's keeping my people apart
Then I'd lead him to my grandmothers house
Where a decent dog wouldn't hide.

Then I'd take him to the Northside
And let him see the prosperity
Along with the wealth of those that got
When the getting was good
Yet, others were forced to live
In something equal to a chicken coop.

Oh' if I could only meet
Old Master Jesus
I'd catch him by the hand
And lead him
Once again, to the Southside
And let him rest a while.

Then I'd tell
Old Master Jesus
I believe I'm getting tired

Of hearing all these lies
About Human Rights;
Women Rights and Civil Rights;
And listening to all their lies
About how they apologize.

You see my mother use to pray
As she looked up in the sky
And said my FATHER
Was going to set this world on fire.
Well I guess
Then Master Jesus
The rich won't have a home
And the poor won't have to mourn!

28

Poem of History

G. B. R.

Poem Of History

My name is brother Rhynes
If I'm lying, I'm dying
And dying, is not a crime.
So back up your mind
Turn it around
Its been twisted
A little too long now.

So come on, pick-up your step
Stretch out your hand
Raise your head
Like a TRUE – black man!

Dig deep,
Within your own mind
Because it's not a crime
Not –to be blind.

So, look around
Don't be a clown
Find out---what's going down.

You see, the peak of the pyramid,
Didn't come from the peak
But from the power, wisdom
And knowledge beneath.

So, Black man,
Black woman,
Stay on your feet,
And Defeat, defeat.

So you can reach out—deep
Into the peak of the pyramid,
Called the brain, and stake your claim.
So don't imitate, but elevate
Like I say, My name
Is Brother Rhynes.

If, I'm lying
I'm dying, realizing,
It's not a crime
To carve out from the –mountaintop
A little piece of the rock,
That you can call your own!

So before—they lay you down
Beneath the ground, do something good.

29

A SPECIAL PRAYER

THE PLUMBLINE OF TRUTH

Special Prayer

O' Lord, as we are gathered here today
Under the canopy of heaven
Asking that you regulate our lives
By the plumbline of justice.

Ever squaring our actions by the square of virtue
That when you call us;
We will be ready to meet all men on the level
While standing on the square, which is your word.
That has empowered us to treat our neighbors
As we ourselves wish to be treated.

Again, O Lord, as we are gathered here today
Under the canopy of heaven
In the brightness of your Holy and Righteous Word
That shines far greater than the noonday sun.

Wherein we see and understand with the third eye that transmits
The flow of spiritual knowledge upon the frequency that elevates
The minds of men that no seen or unseen force
Is capable of deterring us
From your holy, righteous, and divine path.

That you set before us after placing us
Upon the Trestle board of your own hand
And directed us, shaped us, and molded us into perfect stones
That we maybe worthy, ready, and well qualified
To be fitted into your Holy and Everlasting Temple above

Where all your Righteous and Holy servants seek to gain admission
By the benefit of the password of Holiness that turns the lock

On the door of the East Gate
That leads into the temple of eternal rest

Where you, GOD

The SUPREME GRAND ARCHITECT of the universe resides

In that undiscovered country
To whom born no traveler returns
And all the CHILDREN of God Said.
    AMEN.

About The Author

George Boston Rhynes born in South GA was reared by his grandparents Howard and Eliza Bryant. He is a community activist, a minister, and a retired veteran who has traveled overseas to such places as Okinawa, Japan, Guam, Thailand and many other countries. He is the author of several writings and has received recognition from many areas of the country. Mr. Rhynes, still resides in South GA, however he is a traveler spending time with family and friends and helping others.

www.ingramcontent.com/pod-product-compliance
Lightning Source LLC
Chambersburg PA
CBHW050521100526
44581CB00002B/58